Lakdhas Wikkramasinha

EDITED BY
APARNA HALPÉ AND MICHAEL ONDAATJE

With translations from the Sinhala by
UDAYA PRASHANTHA MEDDEGAMA

NYRB/POETS

 NEW YORK REVIEW BOOKS   *New York*

THIS IS A NEW YORK REVIEW BOOK
PUBLISHED BY THE NEW YORK REVIEW OF BOOKS
207 East 32nd Street, New York, NY 10016
www.nyrb.com

Library of Congress Cataloging-in-Publication Data
Names: Wikkramasinha, Lakdhas, 1941–1978, author. | Ondaatje, Michael,
    1943– editor, writer of foreword. | Halpé, Aparna, editor, writer of
    introduction. | Mäddēgama, Udaya Praśānta, translator.
Title: Lakdhas Wikkramasinha / by Lakdhas Wikkramasinha; edited by
    Michael Ondaatje and Aparna Halpé; foreword by Michael Ondaatje;
    introduction by Aparna Halpé; translated by Udaya Prashantha
    Meddegama.
Description: New York: New York Review Books, [2023] | Series: New York
    Review books poets | Identifiers: LCCN 2022029488 (print) |
    LCCN 2022029489 (ebook) | ISBN 9781681377346 (paperback) |
    ISBN 9781681377353 (ebook)
Subjects: LCGFT: Poetry.
Classification: LCC PR9440.9.W657 S45 2023 (print) | LCC PR9440.9.W657
    (ebook) | DDC 821/.914—dc23/eng/20220908
LC record available at https://lccn.loc.gov/2022029488
LC ebook record available at https://lccn.loc.gov/2022029489

ISBN 978-1-68137-734-6
Available as an electronic book; 978-1-68137-735-3

Cover and book design by Emily Singer

Printed in the United States of America on acid-free paper.
10 9 8 7 6 5 4 3 2 1

NEW YORK REVIEW BOOKS
POETS

LAKDHAS WIKKRAMASINHA (1941–1978) was a bilingual Sri Lankan poet, renowned for his work in English, who also wrote experimental poetry in Sinhala. He was educated at S. Thomas' College, Mount Lavinia, and briefly studied law before becoming an instructor in English at what would later become the University of Kelaniya. Between 1965 and 1977, he published eight volumes of poetry. His work also appeared in *Madrona*, *Eastern Horizon*, *Outposts*, *University of Chicago Review*, as well as other local and international journals. At age thirty-six, he died by drowning.

APARNA HALPÉ is a poet, scholar, and musician who lives in Toronto, Canada. Her work on contemporary post-colonial fiction has appeared in numerous scholarly publications. She is the author of *Precarious*, a collection of poems.

MICHAEL ONDAATJE is the author of seven novels, most recently *Warlight*; many books of poetry; and a memoir, *Running in the Family*. He lives in Toronto, Canada.

UDAYA PRASHANTHA MEDDEGAMA was the first to translate Wikkramasinha's Sinhala poems and is the author of the first critical evaluation of this work, published in *New Ceylon Writing* in 1979.

In celebration of the GotaGoGama Library

...A poem contains nothing
but the bones of the dead.
& the bones of the dead, my friend,
do not last forever.

—LAKDHAS WIKKRAMASINHA,
"Luís de Camões"

Contents

HAND BOMB ET CETERA

WE HAD BOTH GONE to the same school as young boys, boarded at S. Thomas' College, Mount Lavinia, but I would not discover that until I was older, in my thirties, when I returned to Sri Lanka after being away for a long time. By then I had already heard of him as a poet. But it was only after meeting Ian Goonetilleke, who was the librarian at the University of Peradeniya, that I heard more. Ian and I had written to each other over the years, and it was during my return visit that he told me that Lakdhas Wikkramasinha and I had gone to the same school, and that he had become a remarkable poet. Goonetilleke gave me a list of his collections, beginning with *Lustre* in 1965, and he told me about Wikkramasinha's early death by drowning. These stark facts about him, a man who was only ten years older than me.

I found a copy shortly afterwards of *(O Regal Blood)* and immediately fell in love with his work, with his craft, that ranging troublesome voice, his radical as well as informal vision of what poetry should and could be in Sri Lanka. I read all of his collections over the next few months and would often return to them—brilliant, disturbing, lyrical. But it has only been in these last few years, working with Aparna Halpé and seeing all the poems in this collection now gathered in one place, that I truly was overwhelmed by the range of Wikkramasinha's work and by its determined political focus. The poems were no longer spread out in small press editions, all published in Sri Lanka, with a few poems rarely appearing in the West. Now, seeing all of them together suggested the determined direction of his work. There is a remarkable complexity of forms, where a harsh language clashes with heartbreaking tenderness. So that we as readers begin to feel that we were no longer safe or even innocent in the world he is writing about, as in "Don't Talk to Me About Matisse," which opens the second section of this volume:

Don't talk to me about Matisse, don't talk to me
about Gauguin, or even,
the earless painter Van Gogh,
& the woman reclining on a blood-spread...
the aboriginal shot by the great white hunter Matisse
. . . .
Talk to me instead of the culture generally—
how the murderers were sustained
by the beauty robbed of savages: to our remote
villages the painters came, and our white-washed
mud-huts were splattered with gunfire.

◆ ◆ ◆

The first section in this collection is titled "Camões: A History," after the poem by the same name, and within it we see Wikkramasinha drawing on historical material as far back as the twelfth century, up to more personal contemporary poems influenced by his own harsh historical times. Gradually, as this section progresses, we hear a merging of many voices into a single poem, as the contemporary voice takes over in "Nossa Senhora dos Chingalas":

Here there is no Christ; we see no Christ—
Christ, with a hair-knot against the strident
Green vegetation, standing; speaking
In the soul's dialect;
Christ, in a Jesuit's hood
Sweating under the flat sun's architecture—

Here there is only a family of crosses—
Of generations dead, and nothing alive;
Nothing. But larger than the dead dust,
Larger than any grave, figures—sweat and dust
In the quarries of laterite, toil.

Nothing: There is no Christ from eight to five o'clock;
Or perhaps only a Christ of fate—
The men cut the brick out of the ground;
The women take them on their heads
To the lorries of the construction yards
Waiting by the old gate—

And I have seen, in the eyes of these women
Burn no supernatural love; but still
Any one of them is our senhora

In the shadow of whose husked feet
The work may stop, the men recline.

But sometimes Wikkramasinha will move into a more
lyrical and hopeful voice, as he does in "From the Life of the
Folk-Poet Ysinno," where we hear a softer debate, built
tenderly with the distinct names of individuals and place.

Ysinno cut the bamboo near Haniketta,
And from those wattles made his hut
And had nothing to cover it with, nothing
Like a hundred and sixty
Bales of straw.

So he made his way to the Walauva at Iddamalgoda
And to the Menike said how poor he was,
And how from his twenties he had made those lines
    of song
Swearing before her all his fealties.
So she said, Wait for the yala
Harvest and take the straw.

Ysinno said, O the rains are coming near,
My woman fretting, her kid will get all wet.

Then the kind Menike said, O then
You take what straw you need from the behind shed.
And Ysinno being a folk-poet, and his lines being not
    all dead,

The benison of the Menike of Iddamalgoda
Lives even today.

In other poems, Wikkramasinha often celebrates or invokes his literary heroes Mandelstam, García Lorca, or Vidyapati, the Maithili and Sanskrit poet. "In Ancient Kotmale" is a humorously exaggerated version of a well-known poem by Yeats. As the book progresses, we witness how his poems focus on more contemporary and personal histories, referring to "my ancestors" or "recollections of my grandmother," and the enigmatic poem "Wedding Night." The present and past are now everywhere, as in the last part of "Poem with a Grimace," which appears in the final section of this collection:

All that I have of you—
a picture: three sisters, a father & your dead mother,
this evening, as always, they must
wear their fine masks of derision,
twisted with lies—But your impossibly antique
features, the time-shaped
purest flesh under your dress
once held in my hands, jabbed at
like a woodpecker, was my
inheritance.
                    One day perhaps
a poet will speak
your splashing arms, of the dead
man who wrote the green
columnar plantain trees

. . . .

I think the river-lamp's gone dead that I
carry to light the small
anecdotes swimming inside
my head—Mandelshtam, beaten to his knees
in prison, is what I wanted to say—is dead.

. . . .

Wars fought then were different, but they
still go on—They still

go on.

♦   ♦   ♦

In this final section, we see the old historical vices still exist-
ing, as in "The Death of Ashanti," "To My Friend Aldred,"
or even in the portrait of S. Thomas' College ("1950–1959"),
where "beaten with their sticks" he remembers "what la-
ment formed his mind / ruined the heart."

And then, most powerfully, near the close of this volume,
there appears a haunting self-portrait—as if he is caught, no
longer just an innocent in a present history. In "Country
School (1967)," a nervously paced poem, he sees himself in
another role, now a teacher and part of the establishment.

The school lay below the Headmaster's house
and my room in it, surrounded by stretches of
    manioc.
every morning I looked down on the zinc roof
stashed green, before I tripped down

full of misgiving, towards the six hundred
peasants' children screaming inside,
with a headache, and my shirt on which
the fireflies had been spitting as it hung
on the line all night; for every day it gathered
a fine dust of chalk. Red crayon was the colour
they most liked to see on the board—
magpies floated in and out of the light; I was
returning to the language of the people—

. . . .

each afternoon, I was the last to go—
back to my room; everyone drifting past—
I could hang about outside or—, what was there
to do? My anger had turned useless. Only
the voices of children darkened in the distance
as I climbed moodily up the steps to the house
where the Headmaster's wife had burnt herself
in my very room, and died a year ago.

There are so many other moments of self-revelation in
these remarkable poems by Wikkramasinha, where he shifts
in and out of this present hardness—with poems lyrical and
then dark—that become a self-portrait:

That in that year the things he could and could not do
Became a proposition in history; so
Writing his own life
As the life of the country, he became

The paraphrase of it . . .

Now, almost fifty years later, there is little that remains of the memory, or the voice, and the poetry of Wikkramasinha. There is little knowledge of his possible journals or manuscripts, or even remembrance of his admiration of Sri Lankan artists like Justin Deraniyagala and others whose work he loved and championed. There are his poems in English and Sinhala. And there is the memory of him held by his widow, Shanthini Gunawardhana, and by those who deeply admired him, like Ashley Halpé and Ian Goonetilleke, who had encouraged him during his early years, as well as by contemporaries such as Tissa Jayatilaka and Gamini Seneviratne. But his poetry is mostly unknown to the rest of the world. And it all feels like a great distance from the sense of fame when we might today see a youth coming across a statue of the poet Leopardi in an Italian park. The knowledge of Wikkramasinha and his art belongs only to a few. But it seems to me that this boy I had gone to school with had truthfully and significantly caught an era between a hard past and a political present, from 1941 to 1978, where he came to represent in some ways a self-portrait of his time.

Even though, in fact, hardly a photograph of him exists today, he has written some of the most permanent and iconic poems of this country.

—*Michael Ondaatje*

INTRODUCTION

LAKDHAS WIKKRAMASINHA IS ARGUABLY Sri Lanka's most influential poet of the twentieth century.* Wikkramasinha, who wrote in both English and Sinhala, published eight volumes of poetry between 1965 and 1977, before his death by drowning in 1978 at the age of thirty-seven. He attended the elite boys' school S. Thomas' College, Mount Lavinia, and went on to study law briefly before becoming an instructor in English at the Vidyalankara campus, which would eventually become the University of Kelaniya.

Wikkramasinha formed lifelong artistic and personal relationships with scholars, poets, artists, and activists associated with the University of Kelaniya and with the University of Peradeniya, whose Department of English had been relocated to Kelaniya under the reorganization of the 1970s. Notable associates during this period included the renowned bibliographer Henry Alfred Ian Goonetilleke and Ashley

---

*Wikkramasinha also published under the name Lakdasa Wikkramasinha. The rendering Lakdhas Wikkrama Sinha appears in *Lustre: Poems* (1965) and *Janaki Harane and Other Poems* (1967). In *Nossa Senhora dos Chingalas* (1973), he uses Lakdhas Wikkramasinha.

Halpé, professor of English at the University of Peradeniya, both of whom were early admirers of Wikkramasinha's work and were responsible for initiating the work on this volume with Gamini Seneviratne. Wikkramasinha also encountered other literary luminaries such as George Keyt, Yasmine Gooneratne, and Siri Gunasinghe, whose bilingual work was a strong influence on him. During this period, he also formed a lifelong appreciation for the great painters of the era, most notably Ivan Peries and Justin Deraniyagala. Deraniyagala had such a profound impact on Wikkramasinha that in 1971, four years after the death of the artist, Wikkramasinha published, at his own cost, a slim volume of poetry in tribute to him featuring the work of the major anglophone poets of the time. In his foreword to the collection, Wikkramasinha hails Deraniyagala as the "greatest modern artist that Asia has produced" and goes on to decry the elite foundations in the art world that closed off access to Deraniyagala's art from the proletariat of the "Low Country," the southern coastal Sinhala working-class communities with whom Wikkramasinha felt a close kinship. The imagistic fractures and surrealism of Deraniyagala's work, always set firmly within a local context, would eventually become hallmarks of Wikkramasinha's "immoralist" style.

Wikkramasinha also formed close friendships with students at Kelaniya, some of whom went on to become fellow instructors. One such colleague, Tissa Jayatilaka, described Wikkramasinha as being profoundly sympathetic to the emerging radical-left cause; however, Wikkramasinha felt a complicated nostalgia for his feudal southern Sinhala heritage. He may have appeared to some as an armchair radical, who would berate his colleagues for participating in elitist institutions, while at the same time bumming cigarettes from them. However, in his moving obituary on Wikkramasinha, the great dramatist Gamini Haththotuwegama, a contemporary of the poet, noted that Wikkramasinha spent the last minutes before he entered the water that would claim his life "in impassioned talk about the terrible events at the campus," a reference to the period of student unrest provoked by the insurrection of the Janatha Vimukthi Peramuna in 1971 and its brutal suppression under the government of Sirimavo Bandaranaike.* One might say that Wikkramasinha was a poet enraged with the emerging fissures of class and privilege in postindependence Sri Lanka. A poem such as "The Death of Ashanti" straddles two worlds as the poet memorializes an impoverished girl who is forced into prostitution and commits suicide while he remains trapped in the position of a bystander.

Wikkramasinha's death by drowning was tragic but not completely unexpected. His close friends knew of his habit of taking an evening swim, often after having a healthy dose of coconut arrack, which he would share with the lifeguard at Mount Lavinia beach while engaging in lengthy discussions on politics. One story, most likely apocryphal, describes him entering the waves at Mount Lavinia and drifting a few hours south to Matara, where he washed ashore, dried himself off, and took the train back to Colombo. Wikkramasinha's life is full of such colourful anecdotes, many no doubt propagated

*See Gamini Haththotuwegama, "The Poetry of Lakdasa Wikkramasinha," in *Navasilu* 2 (1979): 24–30.

by the poet, who saw himself as an iconoclast. Nevertheless, a sense of urgency and fate must have haunted Wikkramasinha, for shortly before his marriage to Shanthini Gunawardhana, he revealed the following to her: "I feel so utterly depressed as I have a feeling of dread that I'll be not able to do any work while still there is time."*

Wikkramasinha's words were prescient; his life was cut short just six years later. Thankfully, his prodigious output within the last decade of his life has left us with a significant body of work that captures the plenitude of his artistic oeuvre. Unlike many of his contemporaries, whose writing reflects their education in the most august institutions of Europe, Wikkramasinha's work is local in its phrasing, imagery, and linguistic ruptures. One might read him as a poet of the bus stands and train stations, moving in haphazard journeys through definitions, both of the self and of an emergent nation.

"To write in English is a form of cultural treason. I have had for the future to think of a way of circumventing this treason; I propose to do this by making my writing entirely immoralist and destructive." These words sound a clarion call in Wikkramasinha's preface to his first volume of poems, *Lustre*. Wikkramasinha, who never attained international fame in his lifetime, was already articulating a form of radical protest poetics as early as the 1960s, and calling for a rejection of colonial language, culture, and form. In this, he was part of a postcolonial milieu, captured most famously

---

*Cited by Shanthini Gunawardhana in personal communication with the editor. See her "Lakdhas Wikkramasinha: In Memory" on page 105.

perhaps by the Kenyan writer Ngũgĩ wa Thiong'o, who broke from the English language and chose to write exclusively in Gikuyu. However, much like Ngũgĩ and other writers who espoused the return to native languages as a form of anti-colonial protest, Wikkramasinha's commitment to writing in his mother tongue proved to be sporadic: of his eight volumes of poetry, only two were written in Sinhala.

Wikkramasinha's Sinhala poems pose a unique challenge for any translator, and it is fitting that the present translations are by Udaya Prashantha Meddegama, Wikkramasinha's first translator and the one responsible for the first critical evaluation of Wikkramasinha's Sinhala poems in 1979. While Wikkramasinha was clearly bilingual, his attempts at modernist-surrealist experimentation, which provoke powerful ruptures in his English poems, can appear disorienting and somewhat labored in Sinhala. This may be due in part to his attempt to push the linguistic boundaries of Sinhala, in much the same vein as his experiments in English; however, his cadence and phrasing in Sinhala, which depend very much on a sense of the vernacular, are colored so heavily by a form of symbolist mannerism and syntactical maneuvering as to be resistant to translation. This linguistic difficulty was described by Meddegama in his 1979 review of Wikkramasinha's second collection of Sinhala poems, *Avurudu Mangala Davasa* (The New Year's Day): "These poems would have been of remarkable quality, if not for Wikkramasinha's use of absolutely rare or non-Sinhala words."*

*Udaya Prashantha Meddegama, "New Trends in the Language of Sinhala Poetry: Review of *Avurudu Mangala Dawasa*," *New Ceylon Writing* 4 (1979): 140.

Wikkramasinha's Sinhala poems, however, possess a pith that is absent in his English work, best exemplified in the fractured cadence of local speech he captures in "Hospital Poem":

A nurse covering her face for a joke
tells me
"Over there, in front
the person in the room
is Tota yaka*—
the doctor!
He will fix anything, yes,
for a pittance." This is the ward of ghosts [...]

The cackling voice of the nurse locks the poet in Kafkaesque subjectivity; he lies trapped on a hospital bed, awaiting the arrival of a demonic doctor who will withhold care unless bribed. The scene delivers more than a sense of the grotesque; it is an indictment of the then newly minted public institutions, which preyed upon the most destitute. There is a surfeit in the language of these poems, and through the disavowal of more formal structures, the work could be described as a radically deconstructionist Sinhala poetry. If only the literary climate at the time had been ready to accept it as such.

Despite Wikkramasinha's anticolonial stance, his poetry is clearly preoccupied with the romance of Portuguese and

---

*A type of devil in Sinhala folklore, which lurks near wells or river fords where young women bathe.

Dutch conquest. In particular, one notes a fascination with the tragic histories of figures such as Pedro de Gascon or Yamasinghe Bandara of Kandy, who were born indigenous, or of mixed European and Sinhalese descent, and whose roles within the great canvas of colonial Ceylon were always compromised because of their hybridity. In these historical figures, Wikkramasinha seems to recognize an archetype of the colonized other—a hybrid figure whose subjectivity is necessarily tragic due to rejection by indigene and colonizer alike. Such figures capture the poet's imagination, perhaps signaling a recognition of his own discomforting position as a poet and middle-class radical with roots in southern Sinhala aristocracy. This preoccupation becomes a prominent theme in his explorations of personal history, where we note a paradoxical regard for and disavowal of feudal family systems. A poem such as "From the Life of the Folk-Poet Ysinno" ironically celebrates the feudal system of serfdom and favor, whereas "The Death of Ashanti" calls for its indictment.

Wikkramasinha also writes self-consciously from his position as a Sinhala Christian from the south.[*] Poems such as "Nossa Senhora dos Chingalas" and "The Refuge: Doova, Cota" (a coastal village famous for the Passion plays enacted annually on Good Friday) capture a sensibility and aesthetic that is unique to Lankan Christians. These poems stand as powerful reminders of the inextricably syncretic nature of

---

[*] There is nothing to suggest that Wikkramasinha was a practicing Methodist. Rather, he writes from the position of a group who once possessed wealth and power under successive colonial overlords, but who became largely marginalized in postindependence Sri Lanka with the rise of a majority Sinhala Buddhist nationalism.

indigenous and colonial belief systems, mythologies, and constructions of identity. One notes that "Ascription," the first poem in Wikkramasinha's first published volume, is a translation of sorts of a poem in worship of the Holy Trinity by the converted Catholic Dom Jeronymo Alagiyawanna, formerly the renowned Buddhist poet Alagiyawanna Mukaweti of the Sitawaka Kingdom.

Cultural signifiers of European modernism are found throughout Wikkramasinha's work, often framed within a critical discourse on imperialism that draws clear connections to the consumption of the indigenous other as the skeletal remains on which much European modernist high art feeds. A poem such as "Don't Talk to Me About Matisse" makes this critique in no uncertain terms, as he speaks of "the woman reclining on a blood-spread." However, Wikkramasinha does not turn away from the modernist consumption of the indigenous female body. Poems in both English and Sinhala demonstrate a concern with the brutal violation and murder of the indigenous rural woman, often framed within a psychopathic poetics of male desire.

Perhaps Wikkramasinha cannot help but write about the violence of his times. His entire corpus, from 1965 to 1977, spans one of Sri Lanka's most incendiary moments in history, beginning with the failed military coup in 1962, and stretching through the JVP insurrection of 1971–1972, which led to the deaths of thousands of young people, many of them university students. Wikkramasinha witnessed the strong arm of the government as it clamped down on insurgents at the University of Peradeniya, and he recognized (not without a sense of personal irony) the role of the artist and poet within the revolution as an agitator and a consumer of political theater. Of note, however, is that Wikkramasinha's extant writings do not address the ethnic tensions between the Sinhalese and the Tamils, which were present during this period but were perhaps eclipsed for him by the violence in the southern and central parts of the island.

Among Wikkramasinha's literary influences, one can immediately recognize his admiration for the poets Osip Emilyevich Mandelstam (1891–1938) and Federico García Lorca (1898–1936), both of whom he translated into Sinhala. Preoccupied with a poetics of otherness, he also translated Umberto Saba's (1883–1957) famous poem, "The Goat," into Sinhala, presumably attempting to make this masterpiece available to a Lankan Sinhalese audience. Likewise, his translation into Sinhala of the Senegalese poet Birago Diop's (1906–1989) "Omen" suggests a preoccupation with the poetics of a nation born from the intersectional growth of modernism and nationalism.

Wikkramasinha has been widely anthologized, both during his lifetime as well as posthumously. Scholars and critics of Sri Lankan literature describe him as "the most original" of the poets of the late twentieth century, frequently comparing him to Patrick Fernando and Yasmine Gooneratne. Haththotuwegama said he was a paradox because he was able to "give the [English] medium...an unexpected strength, by imparting to it the full vigour of his personality."[*]

[*]Gamini Haththotuwegama, "Review of Navasilu 1," Tribune 22, no. 12 (1977).

Haththotuwegama also recognized that the force of Wikkramasinha's poetry stemmed from his recognition of colonial betrayal, "from his response to a whole culture and civilization that had made him also commit, as he thought, 'cultural treason.'"[*]

Thiru Kandiah's nuanced analysis of Wikkramasinha's "Lankan English" demonstrates that the linguistic constructions espoused by the poet create "the general effect" of local speech but are not necessarily reflective of actual linguistic features.[†] Wikkramasinha was not bound by rules of speech in his poetry but could nevertheless mimic the form to produce the exact tenor and cadence he wished to invoke.

The critical reception briefly touched on here has focused almost exclusively on Wikkramasinha's poems in English. His Sinhala poems garnered minimal critical attention and were frequently dismissed as "far inferior to his English poetry."[‡] This critical response has perhaps been propagated out of a desire to read the Sinhala poems as refractions of the English ones, which ignores the fact that it is in the Sinhala poems that Wikkramasinha delivers his most pointedly "immoralist and destructive" work—an approach he declared in *Lustre* to be his contribution to decolonizing Lankan poetics. We hope that our selection of Wikkrama-

---

[*]Gamini Haththotuwegama, "The Poetry of Lakdasa Wikkramasinha," *Navasilu* 2 (1979): 24–30.

[†]Thiru Kandiah, "Linguistic Self-Expropriation in Sri Lankan Creative Writing in English," *Journal of South Asian Literature* 22, no. 1 (1987): 85–93.

[‡]D.C.R.A. Goonetilleke, "Sri Lankan Literature in English and the Changing Faces/Phases of Nationalism," *Journal of South Asian Literature* 31/32, nos. 1/2 (1996/1997): 251.

sinha's Sinhala poems will enable a renewed critical engagement with this work and encourage its inclusion as part of the modern Sinhala poetic canon.

—*Aparna Halpé*

THIS VOLUME BRINGS TOGETHER for the first time a richly representative selection of Lakdhas Wikkramasinha's poetry from the entirety of his published corpus. The project was begun by Ian Goonetilleke and Ashley Halpé, with the assistance of Tissa Jayatilaka and Gamini Seneviratne, and was completed by Aparna Halpé and Michael Ondaatje. Wikkramasinha self-published his poems in single editions with small regional printing houses in Kandy or Colombo, making his books difficult to locate. Only a handful of his poems reached an international audience through journals and anthologies. This volume provides a comprehensive selection of works in English by this major poet and, for the first time, a representative selection of his Sinhala poems in English translations by Udaya Prashantha Meddegama. The poems are not grouped chronologically, but thematically into three sections, each titled after an iconic and representational poem. The first, "Camões: A History," includes poems on Lankan precolonial and colonial history, as well as on rural and middle-class life. The second, "Hand Bomb Et Cetera," provides a riveting portrait of a nation in the chaos of insurgency and social upheaval. The third, "Stones of Akuretiye Walauva," depicts his fascination with familial and feudal traditions. The brief endnotes for some of the poems were provided by the editors as an attempt to draw a thread between the poems and the histories they illuminate, highlighting a sense of internal debate with history that we feel was a central preoccupation for Wikkramasinha.

All of the poems collected here first appeared in the self-published volumes listed at the end of this collection, except the following: "Recipe for a Sinhalese Novel" was first published in *Journal of South Asian Literature* 12 (Fall/Winter 1976) titled *The Poetry of Sri Lanka*, guest edited by Yasmine Gooneratne. "Coconuts" was first published in *Twelve Poems for Justin Deraniyagala, 1903–1967* (Kandy: Ariya Press, 1971), which Wikkramasinha edited. "Poem for a Jubilee" was first published in the satirical magazine *Between the Lines*, no. 1 (Colombo), March 1981, and subsequently appeared in a chapbook edited by Jean Arasanayagam called *Broadsheet I* (Kandy: ACLALS, July 1987).

All the poems in Sinhala collected here were translated by Udaya Prashantha Meddegama, except "Beside Apollinea" and "Tomorrow" (from *Janaki Harane and Other Poems*), which were translated by Aparna Halpé.

ACKNOWLEDGMENTS

THE EDITORS AND TRANSLATOR would like to thank R. Cheran, Sandagomi Coparahewa, Madhubhashini Dissanayaka Ratnayake, Yolani Fernando, Ru Freeman, Maryse Jayasuriya, Lucas Klein, Ellen Levine, Chandani Lokugé, Vidyan Ravinthiran, Dominic Sansoni, Gamini Seneviratne, Malinda Seneviratne, Sumathy Sivamohan, Linda Spalding, and Vivimarie Van Der Poorten. To Shanthini Gunawardhana and Shirani Malkanthi Wickramasinghe, thank you for affording us the opportunity to share Lakdhas's poetry with the world. To Tissa Jayatilaka, thank you for the memorable conversations about Lakdhas. To Kokmaduwe Palitha Liyanage, thank you for the time spent on research at the H.A.I. Goonetilleke Collection at the University of Peradeniya, and for formatting and editing the translations in Sinhala. To Jeffrey Yang, Alex Andriesse, and the team at NYRB, thank you for bringing this work into being. To Graham Sanders, who shares in the toil of all Aparna's projects, literary and otherwise, and who has been a wise artistic partner in this long editorial process, deep and lasting gratitude. To Ian Goonetilleke and Ashley Halpé, who began the work and are no longer among us, we honor your memory with these poems.

Camões: A History

That in that year the things he could and could not do
Became a proposition in history; so
Writing his own life
As the life of his country, he became

The paraphrase of it

—"Camões: A History"

Memorial

Let a few dead names suffice, for the sable dead.
Shot in their compounds, in their funereal gardens
Suddenly bereft of canna, and the odours of
Picca-mal; and the pullulating dust, wailed with sorrows;
Now these words carry no purple menaces
And cry we, in annals and avalanches
For Singho Appu, Siman, Jiris and Punchi Nilame
For Ampe Romanis and the lady Sabarath Etana
Who sowed her fiftieth year,
Reaping paddy in fields enflamed with sun;
For those shot on the banks of the Algoda River
For those who were flogged in the somnolence of the Kelani
For those driven and shot on the Wanawaha rail-track
That rode the sovereign trains of cinnamon

Of tea, coffee and cinnamon, that are acrid memories
In the night death struck our folk down
And desecrated us. Death, at the hand of Moor
And Sepoy had more candour than its aftermath;
Our Memorials walked,
Sewn fast to the shoes of our greatest patriot
Not passing the cunning corridors, the pallor
Of Ministers and Parliament;
Death, swiftly dealt
Had more reality that the indolence
And disorder of our villagers; divided and ruled
Were the scum and the Moor aboriginals
Unpunished the evil, and ourselves unheard;
The dead, in melody of jasmines, dead
In graves unknown.

From the Twelfth Century

Because of the Kali era
because of the idea of a poem,
from word
to word

Nailed on the cross,
possessed,
these are poems written
on a red, blue, and black robe

12 වෙනි සියවසේ සිට

කලී කාලේ හේතුවෙන්
කවියේ අදසින්
වචනෙන්
වචනෙට

කුරුසයේ ඇන ගැසී
පරල වී
රතු නිල් හා කලු සිව්රක
ලියන කව්.

Dandhabanavaka

from a tenth-century bas-relief

Enclosed world: in its duplicity
It is drawn with long red female hair
Over a glaring lake;
Its carved wings flutter in disused time—
Its feet are caught in a staircase of branches—
In a ruched spiral, or a
Monstrous climbing eye.

Camões: A History

Ensaboar a cabeça do asno, perda do sabão etc. So

His name we would have now forgotten if,
In 1550, he had not lost an eye
Which was one half of an open door
To poke the white and red—

When he was drawn across the waters,
Borne down the concupiscent waters—
A heart of albumen, and his mind a coping stone
To make lean metaphors of her repose—

That in that year the things he could and could not do
Became a proposition in history; so
Writing his own life
As the life of his country, he became

The paraphrase of it: hairy genitals
Hung in Ceuta; at night, the jackals howling
As his fingers tapped the skin of time
At his temples—

There was no increase to a man skinful
Of wine, nursing with each stroke
Wounds other than of the skeleton
He lay close to; to a shore of words—

At first on the banks of the Mondego
Drinking the world's great poetry,
The architecture of a kinder world,
The negative Aegean...

Till the swordsmiths grew thin near Patmos,
The virtues they had suffered
Being blown off like the wigs of the Roman Rulers.
There was nothing divine or just

Enough for the Sons of Lusus in that asylum
As the wind blew prismatic over Coimbra.
But the mosquitoes, the mosquitoes in Goa
Shaken from the hoarse scrub at night

Ate at his nerves; acres of hot chillies
Crackled in his half-blind sight;
The wind ruffled like tinder
Across his sentence

On a fringe of sizzling woods; by 1556
Trustee of the Dead and Absent, he was
Inured to the avarice and meanness
Enough to make an inquisition

Of the places he had been in, writing the finally small
Exercises of soldiers
Come from a barren soil...a solitary
Without tropical wealth, till

After so many years here
He was overcome by the fatality lurking
In these waters,
And strove to make an end of it:

The harm done—to separate the crime
From race and God, merely through the carcases of lost names
The bodies, arms, faces of all women,
His indices of a fallen state

7

That his country was at last seen the convict

◆　◆　◆

The convict Camões
Redeemed by his style.

In the King's Jail

from the eighteenth-century Sinhala of Pedru Gaskon

If I noosed at all, it was to try an elephant
If I shot it was at a Royal Swan
If I pleasured it was a Regal Pleasure
And if I died, it was for an High Lady.

Now, for a lady I complete this third month,
Sleeping the nights alone—an animal;
And as the sparrow's belly ripens with paddy milk
and the moon wanes, still darker days await me.

Heavy with Love

*after the fourteenth-century
Sanskrit of Vidyapati*

The honeyed words he spoke
Made my face jubilant,
Thrilled my body, that
It grew and grew and glowed—

My eyes that watched love spring
Were wet with joy; as in
A dream I met the hon-
-ey king, who drew me trem-

-bling in to the red hall
And seized my dress that the
Strings broke with all the weight
Of love; and my hands that

Flew to my breasts fell to
Him, heavy with my love.

Antonio Barrettu

suspended on the road to Colombo, it
remained for a long time in the year 1620
—Julio Firmino Judice Biker, *Collecção de Tratados*

Antonio Barrettu   it was your head
Your head   spiked in the bestial weather
Low as a caste   and the gourd gypped
Guts become the sacked verdure

It was the trophy of the rout
The tongue reeked first   the whole face
Fell in rivers on the roadside grass
From that day in May you had a different territory   mahout

Of war   all fighting done   So
The peasants like flies around the skull
The mat-winged sage of woe
Gather to see the worms convolve

The hive of your rage   Antonio
Barrettu   the derelict fields are laughing
The palm trees serrate the light   below
Is your stoned head   unknowing

The jaw dropped steep   cheek
Bones pocked   "his eyes were blades"   gravid
Holes descant for us the sight
The peasants are   Antonio   livid

Sun of renegades   on the long road
Of fear   you would whelm the heart   goad
Us yet   Without sight   watch   the armies drive
More pleasant cattle to the hot archive

O Príncipe Negro

Prince; priest immaculate; they knew him as
O Príncipe Negro; his countenance grave—
Graver than those of his quivering Grey Friars—
Who renounced no flesh, but his Realm, in Madrid.

And built, in the suburb of Telheiras
The church and monastery, of skeletal white—
For his ladies of Lisbon, in black mantillas—

Above all his beloved—for Our Senhora
Of the Gate of Heaven; and that other kingdom
He left, in the halcyon green salvers of Candea.

His tomb, now rifled, his portrait in perdu—
Only this slight stele after the revolution
And the earthquake; yet the memory of Dom João
Lives, even as his soul beyond the Gates of Heaven.

Luís de Camões

Luís de Camões, spitting in the sea—
slanting—the sea off Galle,
singing of frost over the Mondego: a Lusitanian breeze:
Mondego; frost (you will remember);
a very cold wind, you remember, was flapping about—
you thought there were two winds—
you thought it was like an eel, bleeding—
But really, the wind was very still
that year.

And then
the gaiety of the kafferinha,
& the fledgling gull
dead on the topmast . . . : so the tragedy
begat! O LUSIADS

Sand. Weed. Water. & the sailors as you know
know nothing. My grandfather was a sailor
at 16; a soldier
in the Latin wilderness,
& then he became
a priest. Such ruminations, such memories, however
have now exploded
in my face. 42 "chieftains"
in my distaff
died in the fighting between 1505 &
1630. Luís

de Camões! A poem contains nothing
but the bones of the dead.
& the bones of the dead, my friend,
do not last forever.

Kuveni

While living in the forest of the small enchanted jungle
when raindrops fell all around
among the trees cut down with the teeth of the leopardess
suddenly, I saw the teeth of the "Andun" leopard

They tied roughly the *siddhi* hands and feet
to Hirassakini—that place
where they had to carry her
as they lived by the journey—an animal, she was
clad in a black cloth

As I was not there, at that time, my eyes blinded by
    three-quarters
although milk was filling the breast, tortured in every
    possible manner
was Prince Vijaya who looked at us
Tell us, whether the "thoni" is weeping still in your
    foolish ditch

කුවේණිය

ගිමන් කක්ෂ හිමයේ සිටිද්දී
වැහිපොද හැමතැන ඉහිරෙද්දී
දිවි දලින් කැපුණු ගස්කොළනේ
අඳුන් දිවි කබලක් මට හදිසියේ පෙණුනේ

සිද්ධි අතපය රළවට උන් බැඳ දැමුවේ
හිරැස්සකිනි—ස්ථානයකට
ගෙන යන්නට සිදු බැවිනේ
ගමනින් දිවි පෙවෙත වුනි—සිවුපාවෙකිය ඇ
        කළ සළ්ව පෙරවමින්නේ

හන්දා නැතුවයැ මා තෙත් එවර තුන් පංගුවෙම
        කණකලේ
තනේ කිරි එරුනත්, හැම අන්දමට වද කළේ
විජය කුමරුණි අප දෙස බලමින්නේ
කියපන් තෝනිය හඬලනවද තවමත් තොගෙ
මෝඩ අගලේ.

Hearts of Granite

They took the brand of Cota
to the four reaches of this
island, and scorched the earth from the Four Korales
to Saffragam

in the train of Gaspar Figueira,
in the hard returns of de Azevedo, devastating the hill-
country; in treachery one with the brave lascarins
that saw to the destruction of Dom Constantine

In the voice of the grey harbinger
washed by the seas of Hammenhiel, impaled on
the harshest palm

rotting with the envoy da Cunha
bled, of the thickest leeches,
of the firebrand clan always

for the famed retreat of de Azevedo
the song of de Melho;

palanquin etched with the plum
of musketry, dripping blood on the feet
of the Malay coolies,
on the ravines and defiles; noon,

from within the carriage set aflame—our
ancestor, wan agony not leaving a trace
of smoke in the clear mountains

Ancestors that manoeuvred the grasshoppers on
the deadly mountains of Candea, broke the silence of ci-
-cadas,

    riddled the foliage
and the unseen enemy in a hundred expeditions, crushed

        by falling rock
        poised, like the tall trees
        on the highest mountains

Ancestors like the Fort of Hanwella,
invincible to the hordes that fell before it,
granite as their hearts were
in the plains of Wellawaya, in the wasted Saffragam
the sandy North, that

        deafened to the bronze explosions
of the finest cannon in the world,
opened flesh like flowers screaming

        with the swords most beautiful
      with hearts of granite; so late

they lived in the heart of Don Corenelis

Nossa Senhora dos Chingalas

Our Lady of the Sinhalese

Here there is no Christ; we see no Christ—
Christ, with a hair-knot against the strident
Green vegetation, standing; speaking
In the soul's dialect;
Christ, in a Jesuit's hood
Sweating under the flat sun's architecture—

Here there is only a family of crosses—
Of generations dead, and nothing alive;
Nothing. But larger than the dead dust,
Larger than any grave, figures—sweat and dust
In the quarries of laterite, toil.

Nothing: There is no Christ from eight to five o'clock;
Or perhaps only a Christ of fate—
The men cut the brick out of the ground;
The women take them on their heads
To the lorries of the construction yards
Waiting by the old gate—

And I have seen, in the eyes of these women
Burn no supernatural love; but still
Any one of them is our senhora
In the shadow of whose husked feet
The work may stop, the men recline.

From the Life of the Folk-Poet Ysinno

Ysinno cut the bamboo near Haniketta,
And from those wattles made his hut
And had nothing to cover it with, nothing
Like a hundred and sixty
Bales of straw.

So he made his way to the Walauva at Iddamalgoda
And to the Menike said how poor he was,
And how from his twenties he had made those lines of song
Swearing before her all his fealties.
So she said, Wait for the yala
Harvest and take the straw.

Ysinno said, O the rains are coming near,
My woman fretting, her kid will get all wet.

Then the kind Menike said, O then
You take what straw you need from the behind shed.
And Ysinno being a folk-poet, and his lines being not all
    dead,
The benison of the Menike of Iddamalgoda
Lives even today.

The Cobra

Your great hood was like a flag
hung up there
in the village.
Endlessly the people came to Weragoda—
watched you (your eyes like braziers),
standing somewhat afar.
They stood before you in obeisance. Death,
the powers of the paramitas, took you to heaven
however.

The sky, vertical, is where you are now
shadowing the sun, curling round and round my mind.
They whisper death-stories—
but it was only my woman Dunkiriniya,
the very lamp of my heart,
that died.

The Refuge: Doova, Cota

Heat lies quivering. Beetles suck.
They suppurate the wet leaves on the marsh.
The marsh birds cry out
A kind of suffering cry
                        to this infinite plot
Of forty acres—a stiff
Axle of the bogs

To me lying in the watcher's half-sunk cottage
Among the divided palms, snag
Watching

Above my face, drops of water, hook
Hobble, countermarch

Or at the rising of the wind, the tails
Of water swish—
The grass, in the low daylight, grown like sleep
On our sensations: the suborned dead

A dead family is
All that's here

Without the peaceful promises of the dead.
They interrupt nothing
As the dull taws weep
In the quarries of laterite, the staked

Old blood.

In Ancient Kotmale

In the beautiful principality, in Kotmale
I will build my house of the good soil's brick
With the timber of the ringing forests,
And I will cover it with the tiles flat,
One on one, as the palms of the farmers—

And in the morning I will see
The sun wounded as my heart with a million arrows,
Rise between the mountain ranges
And spread in the green valley its golden blood.

And I will go into the fields in the seasons—
I will sow the grain, a stream between my hands.
I will cast the grain in falling nets,
It will stream around the calves of maidens
From the viridian fire of that clay.

And in the kilns of my sun-wed fields,
And under the haven of passing clouds
As I repose, in those almost everlasting days,
In the time ordained, in green calendars
Will come my yearned harvest.

The Silambari Design

On a copper plate a wiggus
& a quarter wide, a span
and a quarter
long...twelve
hands, sixty
cobra-hoods, surrounded by us, all
of us—the woman with tangled hairlocks I noticed.
—On a Sunday gave her the figure as a protection:

No longer fear
elephants, wild
buffaloes, bears, crocodiles, serpents
& the 79 evils—

I learned it
at Kirindagala
in the Vanni
hat pattu...poor
jungle folk—
they called it
the Silambari design.

The Good Painter

after an Aztec folk song

The Good Painter
black, red
by the wisdom of paint
shows

creamy milk
on the wall
the real world
with a divine heart
perceiving
Jataka tales, all five hundred and fifty-
four
with a faithful mind

discerning pigments
the Good Painter
takes paint
shadows
are all banished from life.

හොඳ සිත්තරුවා

ඇZස්ටෙක් ජනගීයක් ඇසුරින්

හොඳ සිත්තරුවා
කලු, රතු
තීන්ත වල නුවණින්

දක්වයි
     කිරියොද
බිත්තියේ නියම ලෝකය.

දිව්‍යමය හදවතකින් වටහගෙන
ජාතක පන්සිය පනස්
හතරම
ඇදැහිලි වන්ත හිතකින්

පැහැ අඳුනන
හොඳ සිත්තාරුවා
සායම් ගෙන
හෙවනැලි
සියල්ලම ජීවිතෙන් නෙරපයි

The Headman's Son

Menike, says the headman's son
To her absence—
Your note I read with trembling eyes

"He has gone with the cart laden
To the Fair at Aladeni, for two days even
With the elder one"

My heart is fevered with your writing
Menike, I gave the boy two panams,
And he left the comb of plantains you have sent,

And I have your note, love crumpled in my hand—
I will come through your gate
Menike, at dusk, with the kris-knife

May the devas help you Menike! And find you
Sitting, waiting, love
On the half-wall of the verandah;

Menike,
Moisten your lips with your tongue, as in other days,
As my footsteps fall nearer, in the half-light,

And say a prayer
Even as the cart of Siriya has gone
Away, say a prayer,

In my fevered hand is the kris-knife,
And my heart is dead.

Tree Gone Crazy

Lemurs hanging
the tree gone crazy
piling 6,666 bricks around its trunk
that were scattered near the kiln
bringing the talisman

The tree gone crazy
carnivorous birds on the branches at night
waited, perched
smelling the stench of a child's body
the tree gone crazy

A statue creeping,
fallen,
trunk and bark scratched by the nails of a devil
blood-soaked in pain
the tree gone mad

Screaming and screaming

She came in the middle watch
and stood under it
embracing a ghost
becoming the greenest green,
it sways to the charmer's melody
the cobra-like tree!

පිස්සු වැටිච්ච ගහ

උණහපුළුවන් එල්ලී
පිස්සු වැටිච්ච ගහ
ගඩොල් කැට 6666 කඳ වටේ ගොඩ ගසා
පෝරණය ළඟ තිබුණ
කොඩිවිනය ගෙනැවිත්

පිස්සු වැටිච ගහ
මිනීකන කුරුල්ලන් අතු වල රාත්තිරියෙ
ලැඟලා හිටිය
ළදරුවකුගේ මලකුණක ගඳ ඇවිත්
පිස්සු වැටිච්ච ගහ

පිළිමයක් බඩ ගාලා
බිම වැටුණ
යකෙක් කඳ සිවිය නිය පොතුවලින් හුරපු
ලේ වැගිරීලා වේදනාවෙන්
පිස්සු වැටිච්ච ගහ

කෑ ගහලා කෑ ගහලා

මැද වරුවේ ඇ ඇවිත්
ඒක යට සිටි හෙයින්
හෝල්මනක් වැළඳ ගෙන
කොළ පාටටම හැරිලා
නාදයෙන් කැරකැවෙන
නයෙක් වගේ ගහ!

For a Certain Good Woman

The time has not yet come
where instead of us
our kids appear
on the Lambakarna day;
there are many more miles—to walk—hundreds;
fatigue, sorrow
we inherit
struggle and death.

Now, over there
not knowing what life is
not knowing
the date, month, year
not knowing
letters and numbers
those who are starving
agitate.

Over there
office workers
file state papers
into the ears with holes;
from that man's nose
blood gushes—from his mouth:
inside, his mind is rusted.

The big house
now, is occupied
by dust pigeons—
mud walls lasting centuries
of the big house—but in this poem

there are still no transverse beams
the time is not yet up
for our kids to appear instead of us
on the Lambakarna day.

එක් හොඳ අභගනකට

තවම කාලය ඇවිත් නැහැ
අප වෙනුවට
අපේ දරුවන් එන්නට
ලම්බකර්ණ දවසට;
තව හැතැක්ම—පයින් යා යුතු—සිය ගණන්;
වෙහෙසයි දුකයි
අපට හිමි
සටනයි මරණයයි.

දැන් අතන
ජීවිතය කියන දේ දන්නේ නැති,
දිනය, මාසය, අවුරුද්ද
දන්නේ නැති,
අකුරු ඉලක්කන්
නොදන්න
සාගින්නෙන් පෙළෙන අය
කැළඹෙනව.

අතන,
කායිල කාරයින්
රජයේ කොළ අමුණනව

සිදුරු ඇති කන් වලට;
අර මිනිහගේ නහයෙන්
ලේ ගලනව—කටින්:
හිත ඇතුලේ මලකඩ.

මහ ගෙදර
දැන් පදින්චි
දූවිලි පරවියන්—
මැටි බිච්චි අවුරුදු සියගණන් පවතින
මහ ගෙදර—මේ කවියේ
වරිච්චි කිසිවක් නැහැ තවම
කාලය ඇවිත් නැහැ
අප වෙනුවට අපේ දරුවන් එන්නට
ලම්බකර්ණ දවසට.

Day-Dream

The woman lying in bed looking at rafters
morning and day
with blank eyes
the gold coins weeping in my pocket
up and down in the room
looking far from the window
crushing and crushing handkerchief
looking far from the window
living or dead?
Is the heart beating?
In eight hours from now, the day will end.
It will end.
A woman who does not obey anyone is lying in the bed
as naked as her bones. Bones.

දවල් හීනෙ

ගැහැනිය ඇදේ දිගාවෙලා පරාල දිහා බලාගෙන
උදේ දවාලේ
හිස් ඇස් වලින්
මගෙ සාක්කුවේ වැලපෙන මසුරන්
කාමරයේ එහාට මෙහාට
ජනේලයෙන් ඇත බලාගෙන
ලේන්සුව පොඩිකරමින් පොඩිකරමින්
ජනේලයෙන් ඇත බලාගෙන

පණ ඇද්ද නැද්ද
හදවතේ තප්පර යනවාද
    තව පැය අටකට පස්සෙ දවස ඉවරයි
    ඉවරයි
    කාටවත් යටත් නොවෙන ගෑනියක් ඇදේ දිගා
        වෙලා
    නග්න හෙයින් ඇටකටු. ඇටකටු.

Cold of the Kumbuk Tree

Moss
green and quiet
water
floating under her skin
in a jacket
burning like needles

fish with tiny snouts

like a swarm of bees in a hive
together,
suck blood

කුඹුක් ගහේ සීතලය

දිය සෙවෙල
කොල පාට නිසල
වතුර—
පාවෙන ඇගේ සැවය යට
ගිනි දැල්වූ හැට්ටයක
ඉදිකටු වැනි

කුඩා කටවල් ඇති මාලුවෝ

ශ්‍රී වදයක රුනක් මෙන්
එකතු වී, ලේ
විකති.

Recipe for a Sinhalese Novel

Begin in late adolescence, move the hero,
Jinadasa, from the village and the temple,
to the town and the one university, in Peradeniya,
watch his mind watch itself, in graphic words—
Let the male shadow move about in trousers
and the female shadow wear a chequered skirt;
let the skull of the village priest
turn into a small piece of coal
and Jinadasa's mother offer wax flowers at the temple
while the hero goes about the pavements
copulating with imaginary tarts.
Let a dozen letters arrive, like widows, at this stage—
count the pages, cultivate the grass,
water the plants with insanity, and lastly, bury the dead.

Hand Bomb Et Cetera

I think the river-lamp's gone dead that I
carry to light the small
anecdotes swimming inside
my head

—"Poem with a Grimace"

Don't Talk to Me About Matisse

Don't talk to me about Matisse, don't talk to me
about Gauguin, or even,
the earless painter van Gogh,
& the woman reclining on a blood-spread...
the aboriginal shot by the great white hunter Matisse

with a gun with two nostrils, the aboriginal
crucified by Gauguin—the syphilis spreader, the yellowed
    obesity.

Don't talk to me about Matisse...
the European style of 1900, the tradition of the studio
where the nude woman reclines forever
on a sheet of blood.

Talk to me instead of the culture generally—
how the murderers were sustained
by the beauty robbed of savages: to our remote
villages the painters came, and our white-washed
mud-huts were splattered with gunfire.

The Poet

He is the one that, tossing a bomb into
The crowd, takes notes;
The one who, from an unseen distance
Levels on the tripod that black rifle
With sights that see as far as his soul

Trains and levels, manoeuvres for a clear sight
Of the speaker on the platform;
Waits, watching the clock, for the onset of a car
In the left corner of its back seat
Carrying the enemy.

The poet is the one who is always preparing
The ambush, the one who
Covers with layers of
Earth and grass and worn weed,
The spiked pit,
And watches from the level of weeds ahead;

The poet is the bomb in the city,
Unable to bear the circle of the
Seconds in his heart,
Waiting to burst.

Turn Me Over

In the end it is a lawman looking down on me
Encircled on the ground by the feet of a crowd;
And I am trying to say that the four holes on my chest
Do not matter, but please I cannot bear
The sight of this crowd peering over each other on me
And muttering, and the lawman with a small notebook.

So please turn me over on my face
I would taste the dust before I die,
And see the colour of it on my eyes so close,
Hear the shuffling sound of dust
Without seeing the feet of those that make it,
And see so close how my blood-flecked saliva is taken in,
As the earth will take me in—

And know that you see with amazed pleasure,
Four rich red flowers open on my back.

The Mask

My arms are shredded
plantain leaves. I parried the wind
in the hurricane. You laugh:
"Give him one more coconut shell of blood;
he'll run awhile."

I am blinded by the rain.
I am like Kadawara, hung up on your
immaculate white walls—
a show of peasants' wit.

I have lost my country, and I
cannot speak more.
Leeches hang on my face,
jangling on your wall.

They will, falling off, slide over
your polished black floor
to be swept into your
garden.

I could do with a little arrack.
But I hear the curlews shrieking
in these hills. This is a
mindless country

you have hung me on.

Osip Emilievich Mandelshtam
(1891–)

1

In the copper basin as you
bent your face how
the ixora
smelt (or was it
the smell of
soldiers?); &
the maggot-seething
ground, tromped
by soldiers—You couldn't breathe;
not a star
speaks to you. Amidst
that uniform din nor hear
the death-chalked
Aonian song.
Your poems were
ripped to shreds
as the locomotives hooted full
of soldiers in a fit,
going to the "front" encased
in shit.

2

Your skull
was an enormous park, an
enchanted wood
on which the soldiers opened up

before their "heroic"
departures. You only heard
the peacock scream:
it was all a dream.

3

So the wild beginning of night's choir,
the hovering of a native shadow behind bars,
(among a crowd of prisoners, a man filled with song gone mad).

4

You have gone, I know not where
sadly as
the wreaths lie; Osip
Mandelshtam, the choir begins—the music sounding us,

a last good-bye.

The Fugitive

Tonight the bowl's
full of blood.
3 months now, watching
the book-rack. Tonight
I rub the spines of books,
row after row. I need a broom.
I need to push on.

Tolstoy's essays—that Pani loved
so much & gave me; the leaves
stuck fast: I find a red-ant's nest—
small black letters; the slow pulse
of Tolstoy's prose—

Once, I found a plant
like my tongue, called "The dog
with the splintered tail": a hedge-plant & now
off my wrist, a flow of blood. These essays
flow into the soil, my wounded leg billowing out
I remove worms: they die first
a slow death, find no
hiding place. A man lives
to a great age
like Tolstoy. In a fugitive
war like this, there are no
survivors.

Avariya

On a gold plate
like ripe bananas
five fingers
red blue yellow
copper
ash

ඇවරිය

රන් තැටියක
කෙහෙල් ගෙඩි මෙන් ඉදිමිච්ච
ඇඟිලි පහක්
    රතු නිල් කහ
    තඹ
    අළු

Discarded Tins

Of the discarded, empty tin of milk in the refuse
In the rainy season breeding mosquitoes,
Of the discarded cigarette tin, and tobacco tin,
And numerous other tins, are made the last
Returns of the community of the slums
To their fortunate urban brothers,
And their own rich brothers,
And their enemies who masquerade with their women

Without having to pay ten rupees or fifteen or twenty or
    two—
For them are the numerous discarded tins
Taken into the backroom of this tenement and this hovel,
And this gaudy mansion of the businessman
With his five women with huge bellies—
For them are held in these tins now sleek and silver,
Wrapped in paper, the terrible explosions that must
    happen—

And continually happen in the wrong places.

Hospital Poem

I remember, I remember quite well
—Siri Gunasinghe

Yes,
when you wake with the poison you drank at your throat
I remember quite well
how I walked in Kali's hospital
as a guest
Let's go again
on a path in the middle of suffering, in an old clan
the legs
in this ward
in this

ward—on shelves hang—hands;
in this ward, in the glass boxes, still
eyes; in this ward, the nameless bodies—
yours, mine…

In this ward, really soft
breasts; here,
the fingers ward—So

A nurse covering her face for a joke
tells me
"Over there, in front
the person in the room
is Tota yaka—
the doctor!
He will fix anything, yes,
for a pittance." This is the ward of ghosts: life—So
that day to me—through the chest to the heart—because life
was not enough

The nurses, smiling lovingly,
gave me a glass of blood to drink
I remember well

ඉස්පිරිතාලෙ කවිය

'මට මතකයි, මට හොඳටම මතකයි'
සිරි ගුනසිංහ

ඔව්
කරමලේ ළඟට විස බී නැඟිටුනහම
මට මතකයි, හොඳටම
කාලියගෙ ඉස්පිරිතාලෙ ඇවිද හැටි
අමුත්තෙක් හැටියට
        දැන් අපි නැවත යමු
දුක මැද මාර්ගයක, පරණ වංශයක
මේ
වාට්ටුවේ
කකුල්
මේ

වාට්ටුවේ—රාක්ක වල එල්ලලා—අත් ;
මේ වාට්ටුවේ වීදුරු පෙට්ටිවල තැත්පත්
ඇස් ; මේ වාට්ටුවෙ නම් නැති අයගෙ කඳන්
ඔබගේ මගේ...

මේ වාට්ටුවේ හැබෑට මෙලෙක්
පියයුරු ; මෙතන
අඬගුලි වාට්ටුව—ඉතින්

ඉතින්
විහිළුවක් හැටියට මුහුණු වසාගෙන ඇති
හෙදියන් මට කියනවා
'ඔය ඉස්සරහ
'කාමරේ ඉන්න
'තොට යකා—
'දොස්තර !'
'ඕනෙ එකක් හයිකරල දේවි අනේ
'සුලු කුලියකට.' මේ අවතාර වාට්ටුව : පණ—ඉතින්
එදා මට—පපුව තුල හදවතට—පණ
මදි නිසා

හෙදියන් ප්‍රේමයෙන් සිනහවෙවී
ලේ විදුරුවක් බොන්න දුන්නා   මට
හොඳටම මතකයි.

The New Morning

I see birds—wings ajar. Trees.
Looking through the grass I see
a hole, a grave-side hole—
familiar to the customs of this time;
ageing on the ground, vein-shredded
& nowhere. Once we were,
"eager for life"—

Thickets then; branches
cold & wet. & your inherited black jewels—cicatrices
of history! It could conjure up
a morning that couldn't
be ignored, when our breathing together
was being listened to—

& evening, a taper-lit sleep
till a soundless footfall
unshuttered the sky. A shrub could
civilise your dreams then,
picking flowers for
the passionate jars!
(Insistent now, the shouts of Revolution.)

The rooms were irreprehensible: Calmly
white, a tablecloth laid out:
Your parents coming then—
So many years, & "you had grown up so!"
(—With love, everything composed itself naturally.)

Now, out of the window
a generation is thrown out: smoke—

billows, flames singeing our last words—
people kneeling with hot, wounded faces. Regardless,
we must die
among the high tiles, broken brick, while
the raucous substance of new tunes
come; the bayonet of nostalgia,
the sifting out of

the Nothing-Survival.

The British Council

When they kiss my arse, O Muse
Save me from the clap.

Stones of Akuretiye Walauva

How can I go back
Now among a people who lost their fidelity?

—"The Three Sisters"

The Flames, 1972

I love
sunflowers. Once, my great-grandmother
using
the true colours
of sunflowers bled
from the abraded bark of the
gokatu* tree
painted a bouquet of them
standing in an 18th-century
clay vase.
Since then the leaves
have shrivelled and died. The flowers
are fallen
all over my mind—
My mind cannot contain them. I see
that my great-grandmother
had little, if any, reason
to paint sunflowers
—which, in any case, grow wild. And
my passion
to set fire to things, derives,
perhaps, from this sad
history...

*Garcina morella; or perhaps the colour was orpiment, from
Mada hiriyal.—LW.

Stones of Akuretiye Walauva

Recollections of my grandmother
Of a lineage   silted in the mind
Deranged to the bone
Desolation of time grown old
Now out of reach of scrabbling veins
There is that fever of the brain   lucidity
And flight   she recalls
Verses from that departure
And verses chanted at the marriage of the sister
Verses wrongly made   to bring her
Death   at eighteen
And the spoiling of chains and rubies in the carried trove
Before asylum could be reached   Always
It was flight
From sudden unsettlement   from poison
From that ancient house which lost its hours
And the spirit living by the deciduous river   Days
Were weighed with sovereigns proffered to the coming
Of the evil time   Where are the fields and the groves now
Lying by the skeletal village road
Where the axles of those coaches are for ever sunk now
And the straw and the bony steeds   Now

There is only the fallow smell of obliterated fields
And the twenty-one windows of the house
That looked inwards into poetry   into the courtyard
And the grain   drying in the sun   is perhaps
The last memory
Witnessed   before emptiness pervades
Forgotten time

The Three Sisters

I wander in the alien places, knowing that they were
Forced into exile,
That their deaths were
As strangers under the mistrals' tongue;

Knowing, that they were not buried in
Kindred soil—
In the soil which was always home.

How can I go back
Now among a people who lost their fidelity?
I think of their departure
And the land—
Ash from the pyres of the Southern monks
Settled like a curse on it—
Evil-eyes multiplied—
The land; there

They poisoned the three sisters
To find their
Wells poisoned, crops withering,
Women barren—
The lanterns that hung like low fruit
From the branches of egregious orchards
Guttering—
And now, that sky has stopped
Listening in the night
To the woman who weeps—
O Mother of the Curse, all

Went with the departure of the Muses:
They are so defiantly dead—
They will not be propitiated;

It will never be South
Again—love, in my future time
Of the blossoming mangoes—I must
Find my roots anywhere
Else, in this awakening of senses, even
Among the regalia of the bewitched, and
My exiled dead.

The Waters

My ancestors did not know
so much marsh water.
I think I would like again
to be drawn to the Four Korales
instead of being surrounded by
this stagnant water.

Grass, gathered endlessly on the surface
and a line of coconut trees; husks
and its symbol—a coconut shell
rotting in the soil.

I visit the rain. I have a different
appetite to them. The rain on the grass
moves with difficulty—on a cracked and thrown earth

heaves a chilli-stone—
I walk towards it, and bending down
lay my tongue on it.

It is different now. Who will grind anything
but the teeth of sadness?
My ancestors did not know
the absence of so many things,
and this feeling that one is surrounded by water
that is rotting.

Five Swords

And so today
I took five swords
From the almirah
And put them out in the sun in the garden
In a skin of coconut oil
And kerosene.

                    And their
Haunted hilts, half sun in grass
Unwound no history:
The past had crumbled
With the arms that
Wielded them.
History is nothing live.

I merely
Watched
The metal take
The slow
Pustulant sheen of decayed days, and the hilts

Bear their dead mythology:
To stain my face with the reflected difference
And the mind in a dull track, far
From the fat-retched korales
In which these
And a thousand more
Were cast and tamped,
To cut and hack—

These swords: flow and issue of the soil
Took the stale air; grass
Rifting no new nerves
I think:
The rust shed was of an old order
And not a spreading future violence on the land

Full of grease and
Rephrased tough blood.

Weapons

in memory of Don Cornelius Pinto-Jayawardena
(1856–1926)

One would always
love weapons—as women love
cloth, & some
"with a sociable style"...
but, swords, guns, shedding blood,
& then the rain
following you out,
the grass gleaming—

My great-
grandfather would
almost certainly
have lived
up to now, keeping
his 38 guns
in the house...

—for weapons
have a way of
ensuring one's future...one
breechloader
still remains
"a family legend": "It
could break the trunk
of a full-grown coconut tree"...I
recall these weapons
with pride. Weapons
which have rusted; are broken,
but held in the throes

of the same
blood—

the few remaining taken
as a token of my
life—

I look on them with love—
washing them with kerosene,
sometimes with coconut oil,
handling them sometimes for hours at night
in unbroken chasm

keeping

the wake.

Wedding Night

She loosens her hair, back
to him; going away, it was plaited by her
mother; he remembers a woodapple
he'd picked up only yesterday in the garden.
Inside, it was hollow; he watches
the geckoes hanging on the wall
beguiled by insects—the globe of the kerosene
lamp shows them elongated, and the moths
all furred. The tongue of light goes down
the sea-bed the fishermen howl the night the crow
and the noose hangs down the eaves.
The early blue-shot kingfisher
accepts the gift of sleeping river-fish.
He looks out of the window. Drums announce
daybreak, dead, coppery, adrift.

The Distaff

1

Ravelled, the narrow herb-shoulders; head
decapitated—the wind
stirring my shirt-front, and the priest,
dissembling: Finitude...

Eternity. "They will lie here
ever so," And: "You are not without some
guile." Guile! Here, dust to dust. Ashes bespeak
the fat spindle of dissolution. Thus,

the well-lived.

I keep to my distaff, the seven pure
generations, while the kraits are raftered—
watch our fall.

2

This grandeur comes
of the squid's black ink. Here—
once a month, I laugh at times; cough
such piety; alone, to myself, I laugh at times.

3

—Recall the bin of millet, the fall
of Cotta. My thoughts now

walk too close to the marshes, embrace
too much...

4

The servants had lice in their heads.
Jusey, the driver, is turned ghost,
speaking of some other day
at a dying window.

Not everyone is so famished
for these herds of the past, she says.
I remember. A garden
with chimerical fountains.

Great-grandmother
made a ring of sunflowers, a symphony
of a bowl of fruit;

—the "Comb of Plantains"
fingering the gable-edge...

5

A lot of other light
is creeping in under the door—

I have to forget my cousin
who inhabits it;
the letters, sorrowful, she writes me,
wishing for the last burning seed.

She has never known the like
of a breeze on her stubble.
The gloom clings to her skin
like humus.

The Sisters

They are like effigies
Walking to the very end of the garden;
Towards the fretted shadows
Of the plantain trees—
And a streetlamp beyond all this,
Cuts the air
Like a blade.

And it is a story of your sisters—
My sisters, you say, my sisters—
How ever can I go back now
And face them at table?—
Your lips look like two swollen leeches.
Your sisters walk like effigies
In Holland's garden
And cemetery.

Coconuts

It was raining. We began
tossing the nuts
into little hills—
The beginning of the monsoon. "Enough
that we have plucked most of the trees
in time." She
shook one—holding it with both hands
next to her glistening
head, and the little water
inside it gave a dry
rattle. The plucker said:
"This won't end now
till January, or
February. Now you can't say anything
about the weather"—
The shed's faded red door
was open; with sarongs hitched up
we began heaving the coconut-filled gunny sacks
into it. Lightning had, last night
struck a tree near it,
reducing the branches to ash and exposing
ekels and pith,
both blackened. The lightning
was again flashing about.
"We must go in. It is getting dangerous
to stay here"—
The enormous sound
of the accompanying thunder
filled our ears. Some
nuts were still lying about
on the gleaming wet grass

to be picked later. "Soon the scorpions
at any rate
will be dry," she said,
"and the geckoes
inside the house."

The Fiat Car Near the Firewood Shed

In the seat dripping treacle
while the old leather becomes dust—like abandoned ones
in the broken glass
my limbs are reflected, a piece
of my shirt

a creeper has gone
around the wheel
flowers appear; a mongoose
has made a nest in the coir broom; the last

rusted
nut I
remove with the screw-
driver: and crickets chirp.
This is
not a vehicle,
near the firewood shed
a rotten house.

දරමඩුව ළඟ ෆියට් කාරෙක

පැණි වැක්කෙරුන ආසනයේ
වැරහැලි හම පස් වෙද්දී—අත් හැරිය අය වගේ
කැඩිච්ච වීදුරු වල

පෙණෙනව මගේ
අතපය, කමිසයේ
කොටසක්—

වැලක් ගිහින් රිය
සක වටේ
මල් ඇවිත් ; මුගටි
කූඩුවක් මූසු කොහු ඇතුලෙ ; අන්තිම

මලකඩ
ඇනයත් මම
ගලවනව ඉස්—
—කුරුප්පු නියනෙන් : රහැයියන් හඩ නගන
වාහනයක් නෙවෙයි
මේක, දරමඩුව ළහ
දිරච්ච ගෙදරක්.

Beside Apollinea

Beside
the road that goes along the edge of Modara Beach
there is a house—in the middle
of a garden encircled by a wall

filled with roses
so, sometimes, I go along that road

when I am high
with lips painted red
descended from the lineage of the sun
gazing at that garden

the flowers are like breath itself

Aney, the rose-pink dress has no leaves
and there are no thorns in my sarong either, man
we must both belong to the same
order.

ඇපොලිනයා කැටුව

මෝදර වෙරළ අයින යන පාර
අද්දර තියෙනව

ගෙයක්—තාප්පෙකින් වටලාපු
වත්තක් මැද

රෝස මල් වලින් පිරිච්ච
ඉතින් මම ඔය පාර දිගේ පංගුවක් වෙලාවට

චූන් වෙලා යන කොට
තොල් වල රතු ගාපු
සූරියා පෙළපතින් පැවතෙන
වත්ත දිහා බලාගෙන

මල් හරියට පණ වගේ

රෝස ගවුමෙ කොලත් නැහැ අනේ
මගෙ සරමෙ කටුත් නැහැ බං
අපි දෙන්නම එකම නිකායට වගේ
අයිති.

Umbrella

Shrunken in the rain
like an old man
under death

an old man
made of iron rods
in a black robe

under the sun, licking his tongue
on the main road.

කුඩේ

කුඩේ
ඇකිලිලා වැස්සට
නාකි මිනිහෙක් වගේ
මරණේ යට

යකඩ කෝටු වලිනුයි
කලු සිවුරකිනුයි
තැනූ
නාකි මිනිහෙක්

අව්ව යට දිව උලාගෙන
මහ පාරේ.

Red Letter

The red letter that arrived with closed eyes
in the early-morning mail
       bad handwriting
The red letter that arrived with closed eyes
the crow's hand
to me from Kali

ඇස් පියාගෙන ආපු රතු ලියුම
පාන්දර තැපෑලෙන්
    නරක අකුරු
ඇස් පියාගෙන ආපු රතු ලියුම
    කපුටු අත
කාලියගෙන් මට.

Poem with a Grimace

Today, I must thank you;
wherever you are I know, black
sand's clogged your throat. Look at the sugar-ant—
a terrifying grimace on its face,
wringing its feet, feeding on my memory: all
that I have of you.

All that I have of you—
a picture: three sisters, a father & your dead mother.
This evening, as always, they must
wear their fine masks of derision,
twisted with lies—But your impossibly antique
features, the time-shaped
purest flesh under your dress
once held in my hands, jabbed at
like a woodpecker, was my
inheritance.
     One day perhaps
a poet will speak
your splashing arms, of the dead
man who wrote the green
columnar plantain trees,
of bunches of golden plantains, maybe
of the trembling
finger-like leaves
before your window—
(there were too, two
calamander chairs, a plant-pot & two
dusty hands, with candlesticks
before the piano—your mother's).

Once I had sat on the oldest throne
in the country, heard the peacock scream
inside my head:
I had drunk of the Castalian
fountain the Latin poets called
the source of all inspiration.

They over-rode all that—but your sleek legs
facing me—the landscape I lost...
the endless banter leaping on my shoulders:
swords, guns, the broken shaft
of an impaling stick
thrown in the garage, & ever angry,
your mother's: "We are not criminals!"—

I think the river-lamp's gone dead that I
carry to light the small
anecdotes swimming inside
my head—Mandelshtam, beaten to his knees
in prison, is what I wanted to say—is dead. I

have three book-racks. I go tramping
remote temples now, peering
at old murals crumbling to dust.
The fruitful bats in their screeching concert
never see them as the elephants bring

the rains in. For the monsoons were built
five roofs here.
I see the sun on a red column
& the blue monkey sitting on it.

I know nothing of you—
the guns are ready, grenades piled high, bayonets

gleaming. They say, we are not the first,
we are your friends, & we shall not be the last—
A cluster of areca trees are beautiful
when you come upon them in a grassy clearing.
Leeches suck away the bad blood from my face.
Wars fought then were different, but they
still go on—They still

go on.

The Wisdom Won of Ancient Battles

"Where are you going,"
—"To the chilli plot..." My legs
splayed out like a grandfather's
in the long armchair—like a grandfather
I remain in the verandah, resting—

For already I know
with a knowledge that belongs only to the elderly,
that already
the evil-eyes of passers-by
have split & shrivelled the reddening

chillies: None
will ripen—& I say, in the manner of ancestors:

"Nothing will come of it,"

or remind her that

"We have died
two centuries back!"

But my wife will, of course, continue
looking at such things as chilli plants
with the servant woman,
watering them, and keeping things
generally in trim;
(& some things, I know,
do grow again!)

& the economy is thus, in a small way
(in the small way of a chicken-run,
for instance), preserved—

though in all probability
there's no posterity as I've often said
in such ancient blood
as ours, which cannot, after all,
be repined.

The Death of Ashanti

Nuwarawalauva, Kotte, September 1974

A girl I knew her—
saw her once or twice eating
or washing the pots & pans; used to sleep
on a camp-bed in the hall. She was perhaps used
by my cousin: private in the army,
put to look after the pigs. (He had a share
in the house being the last male
in the line); for the sake of blood
I remember I'd nearly married his
epileptic sister (the one who two months back
set fire to the leased-out firewood shed
in the garden one night using kerosene).
Ashanti was different & I don't know
how many she'd given herself to
to keep alive—
& a two-year-old kid she had; but yesterday
I heard she'd drunk acid, raising a great
marsh-howl inside the old house as it burnt
her insides & she died, a seven-month baby
in her belly; no one even wished to know
who the father was; perhaps there were too many,
perhaps it was my cousin the pig
bearer of a name petering out in such
maledictions. I noticed her earlobes—
they were longer than usual as if
gold rings of great intricacy
& weight had hung from them; & then the familiar black
    stork
danced in the hall
once more, among an army of spines

an army of men centuries old who watched & gloated
as she lay heaped upon my lap, packed
with white seed.

under the nightmare of Saint Thomas he wandered
alone by the hederal walls, by the cold fishes sump

the trees were many, broken-willed
and the canvas-shoed poverty under the grey voice of his
    head was bent

in the quadrangle mocked himself to sleep
how could he say "my brother" to the scum who ruled
    the day

beaten with their sticks what laments formed his mind
ruined the heart, and the dreams forsaken homes

in the haze of pain, under the hoarse breath of enemies
did not the spirit form stigmatic, in his cold bed

alone at the rifle range, arsenic fire at the ritual eaves
drunken masters beat him to the wall

and deserted in the cloister, in the evening of years
how he collapsed in divinity in the angelic silence

To My Friend Aldred

My dear Chap,

In this Kandyan weather there is
no shame in having in your bed
a servant maid—
the same passion moved others too, famous in time—
when there were servant maids about;

      Achilles for one—who gave his heart to
Briseis, a milky slave,
& Tecmessa: enemy blood, as Horace has it;
and Agamemnon fired Troy and burnt his heart to a
cinder, hot for a virgin there;

      and 'though we do not get so Greek here,
we are not to such titillations immune
—being Classical in our Traditions.
And so it is
with you and your Jose
with such long lashes
to whom you have lost your heart.

      And no fear, she is not engendered by the low
at all. Dismiss the mere thought; I envisage indeed
such an ancestry
as leading in its heyday
to some king of these parts, or some
noble lord, or at the least

      some lonely Scotsman in these hills. Else
she would not have such a loyal, unmercenary mind,

or cook such yams, steaming purple
and pots of jak, steaming yellow
or have a figure

       straight out of the old poetry books:
Breasts like gourds, and ripe and Oh
nodding like geese, Thighs
like plantain trunks, and Haunches as a king could ride
on, or Keyt

       And lastly
in this matter of praise, in your fortune—
thick black coils of hair on her head, and Elsewhere—
I mean, all's well
that ends there

And all roads lead to Rome!

The Cockerel

to Justin Deraniyagala, d. 1967

It was
the venality
of fathers
& no nine-farrow

that could wreak
such love: Women:

a brass spittoon. Women,

no longer beating
the washing on the stone, peeling

manioc-tubers & the boilt mush
gone purple

(such women axed once; she was
"with child"). The days abominable. Seeing

the dreaming cockerel at dawn—"He's Mad!" they say—
combing his hair with the cockerel's orange comb.

The rice froths in the pot—
the kitchen-woman unloosening her cloth,
standing naked among chatty-pots,
straddling a coconut scraper... He

lives in sanity.

His eyes—two jak-stones—
turn to cinder in the fireplace.

"He's blind," they say.
"He's now dead," they say.

Dead. The cattle
trample across his hands
of old jasper,

ancient grass,
as all art, deep &

imperishable.

Ascription

from the seventeenth-century Sinhala

I worship
The one Triune God
Father, Son and Spirit
As, like a word's
Sound, Symbol and Sense.

I adore
The Lord Jesus Christ
O plenitude of Goodness and
Compassion! Whose Lotus-feet,
Like a Crown, rest on all Creation.

Devoutly
I adore the Lord
Who like a Flame
That issues from the Sun-
Stone, was born of the Virgin Mary.

—*Dom Jeronymo Alagiyawanna*

Poem for a Jubilee

The air truly green! I wit age lives
when leaves sprout lips on hands and feet
and on the bed; when love again arrives
like a Hot One from the paraclete—

And fills the heart up like an almirah
of honey; bunny, in this falling house
by me, a dragon in the straw
is thy bosom much caught under the blouse

and mine blue titmouse also, with tresses rare
is made into a Sunday of the Psalms
and also with a finger there
is thy weeping angel woken from her qualms
and Thus! Our love makes weapons shear
such antique harvests with old steel—
Desire slow, your belly almost dear
knocks my heart out of the Gentle and Subtile

knocks it oh, I praise a matter of true ease
her thoughts are goode enough to eat in bedde
and by Heaven: I clamour! Let no cock cease
(O gently now) thanksgiving, Lord.

Dead Train

After the pallid turbans of the bar,
After the toddy breath,
I have waited on the rail-track at night
With a knife that flowers at night—

With petals poised to cut
And cup each nipple in a flash,
And make each heart gleam, metallic,
Solitary, to the touch

Of a body, lurching body
With a life that flows out on the track;

I have waited for the dead train to come
Silently to a stop, silently to a stop—

The dead train is a mortuary
That will stop for me and for my deed,

Stop for me,
Fifty yards ahead.

Disciple

That body that you and five policemen
Pull out of the Beira—
That you saw early this morning
Floating in the lake,
Had, at seven o'clock in the twilight
A mind thinking: my loyal disciple follows me,
He is at my footsteps, at my back
My disciple follows me—

But his mind was not too quick
To know, the knife I buried in his back,
His mind was too slow to think—
Like the saffron light I flashed before him,
That I showed the way for him—
For him, for you—
Only the knife I buried in his back
Knew I follow no one,
Knew, and was not too late to feel.

If I Am Collecting Things

If I am always collecting things
In the manner of the sand
Collecting,
On the sea shore
Collecting, the corpse of the dead swimmer
Against the soles of whose feet
There is nothing paler;

Sand, infinitely small
Infinitely glistening on the black skin
Peeling off—

If I am always collecting things,
You should know that I am collecting things,
That are always dead.

Middle

The middle of the night
Was built for two people:
For myself, and for myself.

But the middle of the day is called noon:
Taking in memories of the hot air,
Dreaming in the siesta,

Sleeping alone, with a long knife.

The Deaf Man

He has no ears.
Out of his left nostril
the cobra rears its hood—
Is it, the large hood
of the King Cobra,
or the small one
of the sapinni?

One could only say:
the deaf man goes
among the strewn leaves,
who does not hear
The Message.

Work of a Professor

What does the Professor do?
He plants brinjals
all day because he's too
intelligent
to do anything else.
But he loves his country;
he loves poetry...
—and so the Professor
with his brass
forehead, and his quick and sure
voice, keeps telling me, you'll
never be
"known."

His mind like a bin of millet
and a little boy now
swinging on his shoulder
(with a little brinjal already
in his hand) he
keeps telling me,
I'll never be
known. Among the frizzled white chilli plants
at home, digging and laughing in incomprehension,
I reflect sadly—and feel like death:

I'll never be known.

Country School (1967)

The school lay below the Headmaster's house
And my room in it, surrounded by stretches of manioc.
Every morning I looked down on the zinc roof
Stashed green, before I tripped down
Full of misgiving, towards the six hundred
Peasants' children screaming inside,
With a headache, and my shirt on which
The fireflies had been spitting as it hung
On the line all night; for every day it gathered
A fine dust of chalk. Red crayon was the colour
They most liked to see on the board—
Magpies floated in and out of the light; I was
Returning to the language of the people—

Faces of oval light sidled up to me;
Cheeks curved, and the lonely wind nuzzled
My hair: always the possibility was
That this was not the time; was this
The place? How quickly, I thought, a lesson
In history turned into a story of some hero
Of the countryside; all blood was let
In the neighbourhood. Sir, the bell is
Ringing. I had not heard; I was deaf—Green
Pride of the manioc, brick of the country—

Each afternoon, I was the last to go—
Back to my room; everyone drifting past—
I could hang about outside or—, what was there
To do? My anger had turned useless. Only
The voices of children darkened in the distance

As I climbed moodily up the steps to the house
Where the Headmaster's wife had burnt herself
In my very room, and died a year ago.

From García Lorca

If I die,
lay me on the verandah

The lad eating a tangerine
can be seen from my verandah;

The farmer harvesting rice
can be heard in my verandah;

If I die
lay me on my verandah!

*This is an adaptation of a poem from *Modern Poetry from Africa* (New York: Penguin, 1963).—LW.

ගාසියා ලෝකා ගෙන්

මම මැරුණොත්,
බරාදේ ඇරල තියහං

*මේ අනුවාදය *Modern Poetry from Africa* (New York: Penguin, 1963) නම් සංග්‍රහයේ එන කවියකින්.

නාරන් කන පැන්වා
මගෙ බරාදෙට ජේනවා ;

ගොයම් කපන ගොවියා
මගෙ බරාදෙට ඇහෙනවා ;

මම මැරුණොත්,
බරාදේ ඇරල තියහං!

Tomorrow

Let us distill
the ichor of the sun
and drink;

weave a poem
around the moon. Bitter
tomorrow.

හෙට

හෙට
ඉරේ පැහිරි
වීදුරුවකට මිරිකලා
බොමු;

හඳ වටේ
කවියක් ගොතමු. තිත්ත
හෙට.

Lakdhas Wikkramasinha: In Memory

A HYPERSENSITIVE, HIGHLY STRUNG, and complicated person, Lakdhas was sometimes prone to depression and despair. In retrospect, he had a kind of foreboding that time was running out. He wrote to me in September 1972, before our marriage on December 7th, "I feel so utterly depressed as I have a feeling of dread that I'll be not able to do any work while still there is time. I will first have to get rid of all these feelings of fear and insecurity that have become second nature to me."

Considering himself a genius in a way, he was apt to be sarcastic and severe to his detractors, but not necessarily of long malice. On the other hand, he was a gentle, kind, thoughtful, and witty person. These two sides of his character would come into conflict at the most unexpected times, and for no apparent reason, as far as others were concerned. Thus, he would be inclined to rush into quarrels and be involved in disputes even to the point of violence. This is reflected in his poetry, where pieces oozing with disillusionment, bitterness, and despair coexist with humorous, optimistic ones.

His dearest mentors were Ashley Halpé, Ian Goonetilleke, Yasmine Gooneratne, and Siri Gunasinghe, of whom he talked about in his letters. He was especially close to Ian and Ashley. In a letter to me, he wrote about the artist Ivan

Peries as someone "whom I admire very much and want to write about."

When I asked his sister, Kanthi, if she would like to contribute something to her brother's memory, she said what she remembers most about him was his interest not in politics so much, although he had very strong anticolonialist views and feelings, but a passionate, bordering on obsessive, interest in history. I agree with her. Not the present but the past: personal ancestry and lineage, local and foreign history in general, which are all too evident in his poetry.

—*Shanthini Gunawardhana*

NOTES

CAMÕES: A HISTORY

The Portuguese poet Luís Vaz de Camões (1524–1580) was considered to be the foremost poet of his time. He is the author of the epic *Os Lusíadas* (1572). His work was so influential that the Portuguese call their language "the language of Camões."

IN THE KING'S JAIL

Pedru Gaskon is an idiosyncratic spelling of Pedro de Gascon, the son of a French cavalryman who settled in Kandy and married a Portuguese lady. The young de Gascon was raised beside the future king of Kandy and was noted for his unflinching loyalty to the young prince. In due course, when Narendrasinghe became the king of Kandy in 1709, he appointed de Gascon as his Maha Adhikaram (chief minister), much to the chagrin of his Sinhala subjects and courtiers. De Gascon fell from favor when he came under suspicion of being the queen's paramour. He was eventually beheaded in 1715 for the crime of treason.

ANTONIO BARRETTU

Antonio Barrettu (normally spelled Barretto) was the commander of a small Portuguese force sent by Saint Francis Xavier in 1547 to determine the best political and military advantage to be gained by aiding the warring kingdoms of Kotte, Sitawake, Senkadagala, and Nallur. (See chapter 4 of Paulus Edward Pieris's *Ceylon and the Portuguese 1505–1658*). Contrary to what the poem suggests, Barretto was not beheaded but sailed back to India after a disagreement with King Bhuwaneka Bahu.

The epigraph of the poem is presumably a reference to *Collecção de Tratados e concertos de pazes que o Estado da India Portugueza fez com os Reis e Senhores com quem teve relações nas partes da Asia e Africa Oriental desde o principio de conquista até ao fim do seculo XVIII*, by Julio Firmino Judice Biker (1881).

O PRÍNCIPE NEGRO

El Príncipe Negro, the Black Prince, was the title given to Yamasinghe Bandara of Kandy, who fled the country upon losing the Kingdom of Kandy to King Vimaladharmasurya. He was baptized as Dom João, given refuge and protected by Franciscans, and eventually settled in Lisbon, where under a royal grant, he lived out the rest of his days. He built the Church of Our Lady of the Gate of Heaven in Telheiras as a token of his gratitude to the Franciscans who had saved his life. He died in Lisbon in 1642.

"Candea" is the Latinate spelling of Kandy based on the inscription on the prince's headstone as cited and translated by K.D. Paranavitana: "*Quisacram hanc Mariae aedem fundavit hic Candiae Principis ossa Septiantur*, which translates as 'Here lie buried the remains of the Prince of Candia who erected this holy edifice in honor of Mary'" ("A Church in Lisbon and the Black Prince of Lanka," *The Sunday Times Plus*, 22 July 2007, www.sundaytimes.lk/070722/Plus/pls10.html).

LUÍS DE CAMÕES

The kafferinha is an Afro-Iberian dance form that arrived with Portuguese colonists and eventually fused with local musical elements to evolve into the popular Lankan dance form baila.

KUVENI

The legend of the indigenous queen Kuveni, outlines the island's first encounter with the forces of colonialism. When the exiled Indian prince Vijaya first lands on the island of Tambapanni, he is befriended by Kuveni. Vijaya fathers two children with Kuveni and becomes her consort, only to ultimately seize her kingdom and betray her.

According to one strain of the legend, the betrayed Kuveni calls on the gods for vengeance before she takes her life. Her lament, also known as Kuveni's Curse, is held in folk belief to be the source for all disruptions to power and governance on the island from prehistoric times to the present.

The legend, set down in the chronicle the *Mahavamsa*, narrates Kuveni through the lens of early colonial power structures wherein the indigenous woman is characterized as the untrustworthy deceitful other to the heroic warrior prince.

"*Siddhi*" is of unknown meaning and origin.

"Thoni" perhaps refers to the famous Thonigala rock in the North Western Province, well known for the inscription carved on it. However, here "thoni" could also refer to the *Lathoni*—the lamentation of Kuveni, after she was exiled along with her children, from the palace by King Vijaya. Kuveni's lament and subsequent curse of Vijaya's progeny and people, the Sinhalese, articulates the island's first narrative of colonial disenfranchisement of the indigenous peoples of Sri Lanka, the Vedda.

HEARTS OF GRANITE

Gaspar Figueira de Serpe, also known as the Axe, was a particularly savage captain of forces in Portuguese Ceylon.

Jerónimo de Azevedo (1540–1625) was a Portuguese governor of Ceylon who led brutal and strategic conquests of the southern parts of the island and the Kingdom of Kandy, which he did not succeed in subjugating.

Dom Constantine de Sá e Noronha was the sixth and eighth governor of Portuguese Ceylon, who died in 1630 at the Battle of Randeniwela, where the Portuguese forces suffered a humiliating defeat at the hands of the Kandyan forces.

Diogo de Melho de Castro was the governor of Portuguese Ceylon from 1633 to 1635 and 1636 to 1638.

Grasshoppers were a form of artillery used by the Sinhalese in the seventeenth century in their efforts to protect Kandy from the invading Portuguese forces.

Don Corenelis is the spelling that would be adopted by a Lankan, in distinction to the Portuguese figures portrayed in the poem.

FROM THE LIFE OF THE FOLK-POET YSINNO

Capturing the feudal relationships of rural Sri Lanka, this poem depicts an exchange between a folk-poet named Ysinno and the lady of the manor, the Menike.

"Walauva" refers to a feudal house.

The seasonal agricultural cycles on the island are based on the maha season, which depends on the northeast monsoon, and the yala season, which depends on the southwest monsoon. Ysinno makes his request to the Menike at a point in the year when supplies of produce and goods would be lean.

THE SILAMBARI DESIGN

"Wiggus" is of unknown meaning and origin.

THE HEADMAN'S SON

The panam was a coin used throughout the period of the Kingdom of Kandy (1474–1815).

FOR A CERTAIN GOOD WOMAN

The term "Lambakarna" literally means the person with long earlobes, or the one with hanging ears, and refers to an ancient clan in India and Sri Lanka. The Lambakarnas were retainers to the kings of Anuradhapura. During the reign of King Ilanaga of Anuradhapura, they revolted and usurped the throne, thereby beginning a dynasty that lasted until the start of the Kingdom of Kandy in 1474.

THE MASK

Kadawara, the powerful yaksha, or demon, is associated with the god of Kataragama Sri Lanka, foremost of the precolonial deities of the island.

OSIP EMILIEVICH MANDELSHTAM (1891–   )

Mandelstam's surname is normally spelled without an "h." The title of this poem only includes his birthdate, even though he had already died in 1938.

ASCRIPTION

Jeronymo Alagiyawanna was primarily known as Alagiyawanna Mukaweti, the foremost poet of the Sitawaka Kingdom (1521–1593). He was initially viewed as a revolutionary poet, but Mukaweti eventually converted to Christianity and aided the Portuguese in their colonial project.

THE DEAF MAN

A "sapinni" is a female cobra.

WORKS BY LAKDHAS WIKKRAMASINHA
(1965–1981)

LUSTRE: POEMS
[1965]

LUSTRE
  Ascription
  Memorial
  The Long-Eyes Ones
  Karagala
  I Praise Her and Sing to Her
  The Headman's Son
  Hula Girl
  In the King's Jail
  Anula Devi
  Heavy with Love
MYRHA
  Autumn Noon
  Myrha's Party
METAPHYSICAL POEMS
  A Room of Grey-Doves
  Dead Train
  Disciple
  As I Go Down
  The Moment
  The Muse
OTHER POEMS
  Hearts of Granite
  Hearts like Dead Crows
  Middle

JANAKI HARANE AND OTHER POEMS

එක් හොඳ අහනකට (For a Certain Good Woman)
කුඹුක් ගහේ සීතලය (Cold of the Kumbuk Tree)
කුඩේ (Umbrella)
දරමඩුව ළඟ ෆියට් කාරෙක (The Fiat Car Near the Firewood Shed)
ඉස්පිරිතාලෙ කවිය (Hospital Poem)
රතු ලියුම (Red Letter)
ඇවරිය (Avariya)
හෙට (Tomorrow)

FIFTEEN POEMS (1967–1968)
[1970]

Birds
Stones of Akuratiye Walauva
The Refuge: Doova, Cotta
Hanging Man
Nativity
Antonio Barrettu
Camões: A History
Five Swords
To My Friend Aldred
Dandhabanavaka
The Three Sisters
Nayika
The Wind Flows
Galle—In Memoriam Adeline Berhans
Country School (1967)

NOSSA SENHORA DOS CHINGALAS: POEMS (1965–1970)
[1973]

Birds
The Three Sisters
Stones of Akuretiye Walauva
Nossa Senhora dos Chingalas
The Refuge: Doova, Cotta
O Príncipe Negro

AVURUDU MANGALA DAVASA
අවුරුදු මංගල දවස
[1977]

POEMS PUBLISHED IN JOURNALS